STÉPHANE REYNAUD'S

GOURMET
HOT DOGS

STÉPHANE REYNAUD'S

GOURMET HOT DOGS

HOW TO DRESS YOUR DOG WITH STYLE

ILLUSTRATIONS BY **JOSÉ REIS DE MATOS**   PHOTOGRAPHS BY **MARIE-PIERRE MOREL**

MURDOCH BOOKS

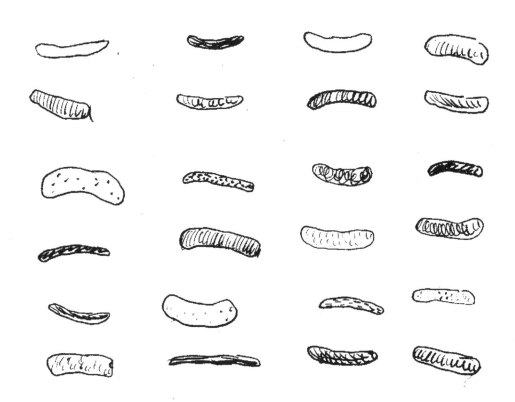

CONTENTS

 RECIPES FOR GOURMET HOT DOGS

FINE GROUND

Hot Dogs & Sausages

COARSE GROUND

Hot Dogs & Sausages

Good company for your hot dogs

The Strasbourg Sausage

The Strasbourg is a smoked sausage with an emulsion-style filling of pork, beef and veal. The sharp 'crack' of the cooked sausage when you bite into it gives it its nickname, the 'knack' (but it's also called the 'stras' or 'fritz'). A true international star, this Alsatian can be dressed with mustard, topped with sauce and wrapped in caramelised onions. It thrills the tastebuds of little ones and enchants those of grown-ups. Always at the ready in many refrigerators (and performing very well at these temperatures), the knack is part of everyday life. It's up to us to make it unique.

If this sausage is not available from speciality butchers or good food markets, ask your butcher to suggest a suitable substitute.

BELLE

STRASBOURG, CLASSIC SWEET AND SOUR MUSTARD AND KETCHUP

makes 4 hot dogs

4 milk buns (see page 128)
4 Strasbourg sausages
2 tablespoons tomato sauce (ketchup) (see page 138)
2 tablespoons Savora sweet mustard sauce (see **note**)

Note: Savora is a French commercial sauce available from some speciality food stores. You can substitute with a good quality honey mustard sauce.

Preheat the oven to 160°C (315°F/Gas 2–3).
   Warm the buns in the oven for 5 minutes. Poach the sausages in gently simmering water for 3 minutes.
   Open the buns, add the sausages and top with generous zigzags of ketchup and mustard. Close the buns and serve immediately.

MIMINE
STRASBOURG, COMTÉ, CRÈME FRAÎCHE, SHALLOTS

makes 4 hot dogs

4 traditional hot dog buns (see page 128)
4 Strasbourg sausages
3 French shallots (eschalots), sliced
2 tablespoons olive oil
Salt and pepper
1 bunch of chives, finely chopped
150 g (5½ oz) Comté or gruyère cheese, grated
1 tablespoon crème fraîche

Preheat the oven to 160°C (315°F/Gas 2–3).

Sauté the shallot in the olive oil over a low heat until well softened. Season.

Mix the chives with the grated cheese and add the crème fraîche.

Poach the sausages in gently simmering water for 3 minutes.

Open the buns, spread with half the cheese mixture, add the sausages, spread over the remaining cheese mixture and top with the softened shallot.

Warm the filled buns in the oven for 5 minutes then serve immediately.

TROPCHOU
STRASBOURG, HORSERADISH CREAM, CABBAGE
PORK BELLY, CUMIN

makes 4 hot dogs

4 milk buns (see page 128)
4 Strasbourg sausages
4 leaves of curly green cabbage
2 slices of pork belly, cut into matchsticks
1 tablespoon horseradish
1 tablespoon crème fraîche
1 teaspoon cumin seeds
Salt and pepper

Preheat the oven to 160°C (315°F/Gas 2–3).
   Drop the cabbage leaves into boiling salted water for
1 minute, then immediately rinse under cold water. Drain
and pat dry. Finely shred the cabbage leaves.
   Brown the pork belly in a frying pan, add the cabbage
and cook for 3–4 minutes. Let this mixture cool.
   Mix together the horseradish, crème fraîche and cumin
and add to the pork belly and cabbage. Season.
   Warm the buns in the oven for 5 minutes. Poach the
sausages in gently simmering water for 3 minutes.
   Open the buns and fill with the cabbage mixture and
sausages. Close the buns and serve immediately.

HOPLA

STRASBOURG, CHOPPED OMELETTE, FRIED BACON
DICED TOMATOES, CORIANDER, DICED MIMOLETTE CHEESE

makes 4 hot dogs

4 sweet milk buns (see page 128)
4 Strasbourg sausages
2 eggs
1 tablespoon crème fraîche
Salt and pepper
4 slices of smoked bacon, cut into small strips or lardons
1 tablespoon olive oil
1 tablespoon moutarde de Meaux (wholegrain mustard)
1 oxheart tomato, diced
100 g (3½ oz) aged mimolette or aged cheddar cheese, diced
4 coriander (cilantro) sprigs, leaves only

Preheat the oven to 160°C (315°F/Gas 2–3).
Whisk the eggs with the crème fraîche. Season.

Sauté the bacon in a non-stick frying pan over a low heat for 2 minutes, add the egg mixture and make an omelette. Remove from the heat then roughly chop the omelette.

Combine the olive oil with the mustard.

Warm the buns in the oven for 5 minutes. Poach the sausages in gently simmering water for 3 minutes.

Open the buns, spread with the mustard mixture, add the omelette, tomato, cheese, coriander and top with the sausages. Close the buns and serve immediately.

The Frankfurter
Sausage

The frankfurter is made from finely ground pork, beef or veal, often all three. It is a pre-cooked, smoked sausage that may contain added sweeteners, additives and fats, so it is important to know exactly what's in it before buying. Sometimes skinless, it can be grilled or steamed and is also called a 'Weiner', 'Hot Dog', 'Frank' and 'Weenie'. The frankfurter is the yin to the hot dog bun's yang, the tenon to the mortise. It is the most popular sausage in the United States. With just a little ketchup and a dash of mustard, it will satisfy the most ferocious appetite.

TOUT DOUX

FRANKFURTER, SWEET AND SOUR SAUCE, SULTANAS MUSTARD GREENS

makes 4 hot dogs

4 traditional hot dog buns (see page 128)
4 frankfurter sausages
100 g (3½ oz) sultanas (golden raisins)
2 tablespoons honey
2 tablespoons sweet and sour sauce (see **note**)
1 tablespoon sweet relish (see page 140)
2 handfuls of baby mustard greens

Note: Sweet and sour sauce is available in the supermarket.

Preheat the oven to 160°C (315°F/Gas 2–3).

Combine the sultanas and honey in a saucepan and cover with water. Bring to the boil, then let cool to room temperature.

Combine the sweet and sour sauce with the relish. Reserve half this mixture and add the mustard greens and sultanas to remainder.

Warm the buns in the oven for 5 minutes. Poach the sausages in gently simmering water for 3 minutes.

Open the buns, spread with the reserved sauce then fill with the sultana salad and sausages. Close the buns and serve immediately.

KEBAB

FRANKFURTER, YOGHURT SAUCE, CHILLI
ICEBERG LETTUCE, ONION

makes 4 hot dogs

4 traditional hot dog buns (see page 128)
4 frankfurter sausages
125 g (4½ oz) Greek-style yoghurt
1 tablespoon mayonnaise
Juice of ½ a small lemon
½ a garlic clove, finely chopped
1 small mild white onion, finely chopped
1 teaspoon herbes de Provence (mixed dried herbs)
1 teaspoon harissa
1 iceberg lettuce (or 3 little gem or baby cos
    lettuces), roughly chopped

Preheat the oven to 160°C (315°F/Gas 2–3).

Combine the yoghurt and mayonnaise with the lemon juice, garlic, onion and mixed herbs. Add the harissa. Reserve half the sauce and combine the lettuce with the remainder.

Warm the buns in the oven for 5 minutes. Poach the sausages in gently simmering water for 3 minutes.

Open the buns, spread with the reseved sauce then fill with the salad and sausages. Close the buns and serve immediately.

DERRICK

FRANKFURTER, SAUERKRAUT, CORIANDER SEEDS SPECK

 makes 4 hot dogs

4 milk buns (see page 128)
4 frankfurter sausages
100 g (3½ oz) speck (smoked belly pork),
    sliced into matchsticks
1 teaspoon coriander seeds, crushed
1 teaspoon juniper berries, crushed
1 glass dry white wine
1 tablespoon dijon mustard
200 g (7 oz) prepared sauerkraut
2 chives, finely chopped

 22

Preheat the oven to 160°C (315°F/Gas 2–3).
    Sauté the speck in a frying pan over a low heat for 2 minutes. Add the coriander seeds, juniper berries and the white wine. Cook for a further 5 minutes.
    Warm the buns in the oven for 5 minutes. Poach the sausages in gently simmering water for 3 minutes.
    Open the buns, spread with the mustard then fill with the speck, sauerkraut and sausages and sprinkle with the chopped chives. Close the buns and serve immediately.

BERLINE

FRANKFURTER, MELTED CHEESE
FRESH ONIONS, BABY SHISO

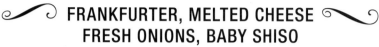

makes 4 hot dogs

4 milk buns (see page 128)

4 frankfurter sausages

1 tablespoon tomato sauce (ketchup) (see page 138)

1 teaspoon tomato paste (concentrated purée)

1 tablespoon olive oil

2 bulb spring onions (scallions), greens and whites
  sliced separately

150 g (5½ oz) Salers or mature cheddar cheese,
  thinly sliced

a few baby shiso sprouts, for garnish (optional)

Preheat the oven to 160°C (315°F/Gas 2–3).

Combine the tomato sauce, tomato paste and olive oil with the green part of the onion.

Poach the sausages in gently simmering water for 3 minutes.

Open the buns, spread with the tomato sauce mixture, add the sausages and top with the cheese.

Warm the filled buns in the oven for 5 minutes. Remove the buns from the oven and scatter the white part of the onion and the baby shiso over them. Close the buns and serve immediately.

The Vienna Sausage

The Vienna sausage is the first cousin of the Strasbourg, or even its sister. Often more slender and willowy, it contains a delicate filling of pork, beef and veal and is cooked and smoked. The Vienna willingly slips into a brioche robe, thus presented in all her finery. She's a socialite who takes nothing to dress and dances with relish—any relish.

If this sausage is not available from speciality butchers or good food markets, ask your butcher for advice, or substitute with a frankfurter or Strasbourg.

POPEYE

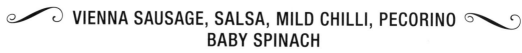

VIENNA SAUSAGE, SALSA, MILD CHILLI, PECORINO BABY SPINACH

makes 4 hot dogs

4 milk buns (see page 128)
4 Vienna sausages
1 bird's eye chilli, finely chopped
50 g (1¾ oz) pecorino cheese, finely chopped
3 tablespoons sauce vierge (see page 140)
1 handful of baby spinach
1 tablespoon olive oil
1 mild red chilli, sliced

Preheat the oven to 160°C (315°F/Gas 2–3).

Combine the bird's eye chilli and pecorino cheese with the sauce vierge to make a salsa.

Dress the spinach with the olive oil.

Warm the buns in the oven for 5 minutes. Poach the sausages in gently simmering water for 3 minutes.

Open the buns, spread with the salsa, then fill with the spinach, sliced chilli and the sausages. Close the buns and serve immediately.

FILOCHE

makes 4 hot dogs

4 sweet milk buns (see page 128)
4 Vienna sausages
4 thin slices of smoked bacon, cut in half
1 tablespoon moutarde de Meaux (wholegrain mustard)
2 tablespoons olive oil
1 French shallot (eschalot), finely chopped
1 tablespoon balsamic glaze
2 little gem (sucrine) or baby cos lettuces,
   leaves separated
2 tomatoes, diced

Preheat the oven to 160°C (315°F/Gas 2–3).
   Cook the bacon in a frying pan with no added fat for about 1–2 minutes.
   Combine the mustard with the olive oil, shallot and balsamic glaze. Reserve half of this vinaigrette and dress the lettuce with the remainder.
   Warm the buns in the oven for 5 minutes. Poach the sausages in gently simmering water for 3 minutes.
   Open the buns, spread with the reserved vinaigrette then fill with the lettuce, tomato, bacon and sausages. Close the buns and serve immediately.

AIETXU

makes 4 hot dogs

4 traditional hot dog buns (see page 128)
4 Vienna sausages
150 g (5½ oz) sheep's milk cheese (e.g. Ossau Iraty), thinly
   sliced (see **notes**)
2 tablespoons black cherry (Itxassou) jam (see **notes**)
12 mint leaves, shredded

Notes: Ossau Iraty is the traditional Basque sheep's milk cheese served with
cherry jam. If you can't track it down, you could even use buffalo mozzarella.
   Itxassou is a village in the Basque area famous for its black cherries.
You can use any good quality black cherry jam as a substitute.

Preheat the oven to 160°C (315°F/Gas 2–3).
   Poach the sausages in gently simmering water for
3 minutes.
   Open the buns, lay cheese slices on each side, spread
with jam and sprinkle over the mint. Warm the buns in the
oven for 5 minutes.
   Remove the buns from the oven and add the sausages.
Close the buns and serve immediately.

NOUYORC

VIENNA SAUSAGE, SWEET RELISH, KETCHUP, MUSTARD

makes 4 hot dogs

4 traditional hot dog buns (see page 128)
4 Vienna sausages
2 tablespoons sweet relish (see page 140)
2 tablespoons tomato sauce (ketchup) (see page 138)
2 tablespoons mild mustard

Preheat the oven to 160°C (315°F/Gas 2–3).
   Warm the buns in the oven for 5 minutes. Poach the sausages in gently simmering water for 3 minutes.
   Open the buns, spread with the relish, tomato sauce and mustard and add the sausages. Close the buns and serve immediately.

34

The Veal Sausage

Often called 'boudin blanc' (which can also contain pork) but also known as 'weisswurst', 'Bavarian' or 'bockwurst', the veal sausage is characterised by a cooked veal filling enriched with egg, cream and spices. She is often favoured during the end-of-year festivities. A little old fashioned, the veal sausage is a grande dame with a reputation for circulating in high society. What a pleasure however to escort her down the street, take her by the hand and nibble her in a corner, throwing off the shackles of fine china to flirt with a paper napkin. The Champagne bubbles have a whiff of hops in that case, but the rating remains intact: a 3-star experience on the footpath.

OLÉ!

 VEAL SAUSAGE, CHORIZO, RELISH, PRESERVED LEMON

 makes 4 hot dogs

4 sweet milk buns (see page 128)
4 veal sausages
8 slices of spicy chorizo, cut into strips
3 tablespoons sweet relish (see page 140)
2 tablespoons Savora sweet mustard sauce
  (see **note** page 8)
1 preserved lemon, rind finely diced
2 leaves of sorrel, shredded
1 bunch of tarragon, leaves only

Preheat the oven to 160°C (315°F/Gas 2–3).
  Sauté the chorizo in a frying pan over a low heat for
2 minutes. Combine the relish with the mustard sauce.
Add the lemon, sorrel and tarragon leaves.
  Grill the sausages for about 10 minutes, or until well
browned and cooked through. Warm the buns in the oven
for 5 minutes.
  Open the buns, spread with half the relish mixture, add
the sausages, then top with the remaining relish mixture
and chorizo strips. Close the buns and serve immediately.

CHILLI

makes 4 hot dogs

4 milk buns (see page 128)
4 veal sausages
1 slice of smoked bacon, finely chopped
100 g (3½ oz) cooked kidney beans, or tinned
    kidney beans, drained and rinsed
2 tablespoons barbecue sauce (see page 138)
1 teaspoon tomato paste (concentrated purée)
5 piquillo peppers, cut into strips (see **note**)
100 g (3½ oz) cheddar cheese, chopped

Note: Piquillo peppers are available in jars from supermarkets and
speciality food stores.

Preheat the oven to 160°C (315°F/Gas 2–3).

Sauté the bacon in a frying pan over a medium–low
heat for 2 minutes. Add the kidney beans, barbecue
sauce and tomato paste and cook the mixture for about
5 minutes, or until saucy.

Warm the buns in the oven for 5 minutes. Poach the
sausages in gently simmering water for 3 minutes. If your
veal sausage is not precooked, increase poaching time to
10 minutes, or until piping hot and cooked through.

Open the buns and fill with the kidney bean mixture,
sausages, piquillo peppers and cheddar. Close the buns
and serve immediately.

PICKLES

VEAL SAUSAGE, CARAMELISED ONIONS PICKLED RED ONIONS, GRILLED SPRING ONIONS

makes 4 hot dogs

4 traditional hot dog buns (see page 128)
4 veal sausages
2 red onions, quartered
2 tablespoons wine vinegar
2 tablespoons light brown sugar
50 g (1¾ oz) butter
150 ml (5 fl oz) water
1 white onion, sliced
2 tablespoons olive oil
2 bulb spring onions (scallions), sliced lengthways
2 tablespoons tomato sauce (ketchup) (see page 138)

Preheat the oven to 160°C (315°F/Gas 2–3).

Cook the red onion in the vinegar, sugar, butter and water until the liquid has completely evaporated.

Sauté the white onion in the olive oil over a low heat until well softened.

Grill the spring onion for a few minutes on a cast-iron plate or chargrill pan.

Grill the sausages for about 10 minutes, or until well browned and cooked through. Warm the buns in the oven for 5 minutes.

Open the buns, spread with the tomato sauce, add the sausages and top with the three onions. Close the buns and serve immediately.

SIAM

 VEAL SAUSAGE, CARROTS, CORIANDER
SWEET AND SOUR SAUCE

makes 4 hot dogs

4 milk buns (see page 128)
4 veal sausages
½ a garlic clove, finely chopped
1 tablespoon Vietnamese fish sauce (nuoc mam)
2 tablespoons soy sauce
1 tablespoon lemon juice
1 tablespoon caster (superfine) sugar
2 tablespoons sesame seeds
3 carrots, cut into thin matchsticks
1 bunch of coriander (cilantro), leaves only
1 bunch of chives, chopped

 44

Preheat the oven to 160°C (315°F/Gas 2–3).

Mix together the garlic, fish sauce, soy sauce, lemon juice, sugar and sesame seeds. Reserve one-quarter of the sauce. Mix the remainder with the carrot, coriander and chives.

Grill the sausages for about 10 minutes, or until well browned and cooked through. Warm the buns in the oven for 5 minutes.

Open the buns, brush with the reserved sauce, add the sausages and top with the carrot salad. Close the buns and serve immediately.

The Cervelat

The cervelat is the heftiest of sausages, the front-row prop of the fine-grind
pack that's made, like the three-quarter line, from pork, beef and veal. It
is cured, smoked, semi-dried and ready to eat. Alsace is its cradle, where
it developed its forward build to mark a power-packed try on the keenest
canines between two pieces of bread. Beneath its thuggish appearance, the
cervelat is a cushion of pleasure. Soft like a full belly, it is the St Bernard of
hot dogs. The cervelat is known as the 'summer sausage' in the United States.

If this sausage is not available from speciality butchers or good
food markets, ask your butcher for advice or substitute with
a frankfurter (but the cervelat has a smokier flavour).

MUSCLOR

CERVELAT, MUNSTER, PEAR
MILD MUSTARD, CUMIN

makes 4 hot dogs

4 sweet milk buns (see page 128)
2 cervelat sausages
2 sweet onions, sliced
3 tablespoons olive oil
120 g (4¼ oz) farmstead (fermier) munster, mature brie
   or washed rind cheese, thinly sliced
1 pear, peeled, cored and thinly sliced
1 teaspoon ground cumin
2 tablespoons mild mustard

Preheat the oven to 160°C (315°F/Gas 2–3).

Sauté the onion in the olive oil over a low heat until well softened.

Poach the cervelats in gently simmering water for 5 minutes and halve them lengthways. Cut each half into four pieces.

Open the buns, spread with the softened onion, add the sausage pieces and tuck the slices of munster cheese and pear in between them.

Warm the filled buns in the oven for 5 minutes, then sprinkle with cumin and drizzle with mild mustard. Close the buns and serve immediately.

CLUB

CERVELAT, COCKTAIL SAUCE
MIMOLETTE CHEESE, LETTUCE

makes 4 hot dogs

4 sweet milk buns (see page 128)
2 cervelat sausages
3 tablespoons mayonnaise
1 tablespoon tomato sauce (ketchup)
   (see page 138)
1 teaspoon barbecue sauce (see page 138)
1 teaspoon Cognac
2 tomatoes, thinly sliced
2 little gem (sucrine) or baby cos lettuces,
   leaves separated
100 g (3½ oz) aged mimolette or aged
   cheddar cheese, roughly cut

Combine the mayonnaise with the tomato sauce,
barbecue sauce and Cognac to make the cocktail sauce.
   Poach the cervelats in gently simmering water
for 5 minutes and halve them lengthways.
   Open the buns, spread with half the cocktail
sauce, add the tomato, lettuce, a little more cocktail
sauce, then the half-sausages, the remaining
cocktail sauce and top with the pieces of mimolette.
Close the buns and serve immediately.

VIVA

 CERVELAT, SEMI-DRIED TOMATOES, ARTICHOKES IN OIL
ROCKET, BASIL, MOZZARELLA

makes 4 hot dogs

4 sweet milk buns (see page 128)
2 cervelat sausages
1 bunch of basil
4 tablespoons olive oil
Juice of ½ a lemon
1 French shallot (eschalot), chopped
1 handful of rocket (arugula)
1 ball buffalo mozzarella, sliced
4 artichokes in oil, sliced
8 semi-dried (sun-blushed) tomatoes in oil
Fleur de sel (fine sea salt) and cracked black pepper

Preheat the oven to 160°C (315°F/Gas 2–3).
   Purée the basil with the olive oil and lemon juice,
then add the shallot. Reserve half. Combine the rocket
and mozzarella and dress with the remainder.
   Poach the cervelats in gently simmering water
for 5 minutes then halve them lengthways.
Warm the buns in the oven for 5 minutes.
   Open the buns, spread with the reserved purée,
add the sausage halves, top with the artichokes,
rocket, semi-dried tomatoes and mozzarella.
Sprinkle with fleur de sel and cracked black
pepper. Close the buns and serve immediately.

ROUXY

CERVELAT, BLEU D'AUVERGNE, HONEY, HAZELNUTS

 makes 4 hot dogs

4 sweet milk buns (see page 128)
2 cervelat sausages
150 g (5½ oz) bleu d'Auvergne or other
    well-flavoured blue cheese
1 tablespoon crème fraîche
1 tablespoon chestnut or leatherwood honey
    (see **note**)
100 g (3½ oz) hazelnuts
1 red onion, sliced

Note: Chestnut honey is available from speciality food stores.
Use leatherwood honey if it is unavailable.

Preheat the oven to 180°C (350°F/Gas 4).
    Mash the blue cheese with the crème fraîche and honey.
    Toast the hazelnuts in the preheated oven for
5–7 minutes, then roughly crush them. Reduce the
oven temperature to 160°C (315°F/Gas 2–3).
    Poach the cervelats in gently simmering water
for 5 minutes and halve them lengthways.
    Open the buns, add the half-sausages, spread with
the cheese mixture, scatter over the hazelnuts and top
with the onion.
    Warm the filled buns in the oven for 5 minutes.
Close the buns and serve immediately.

The Chipolata

The chipolata is no doubt the most well known of the sausages. Long and thin, it's called a 'godiveau' in some parts of France. It is made from coarsely ground pork seasoned with herbs and spices. The barbecue is its compulsory holiday destination. An easygoing sausage, the chipolata grills well, can be eaten between two fingers and goes with everything but not just anything. It's thus the ideal ally when you have big tables to feed.

If this sausage is not available from speciality butchers or good food markets, ask your butcher to suggest a suitable pork sausage or substitute with a Vienna. Not to be confused with cocktail-size chipolatas.

THYMETIME

CHIPOLATA, EGGPLANT, ZUCCHINI
BLACK OLIVES, BASIL

makes 4 hot dogs

4 milk buns (see page 128)
4 chipolata sausages
1 eggplant (aubergine), finely diced
2 bulb spring onions (scallions), sliced
1 red onion, sliced
5 tablespoons olive oil
1 zucchini (courgette), finely diced
1 teaspoon herbes de Provence (mixed dried herbs)
100 g (3½ oz) black dry-salted olives, pitted and diced
1 bunch of basil, leaves only, chopped

Preheat the oven to 160°C (315°F/Gas 2–3).

Sauté the eggplant, spring onion and red onion in the olive oil in a frying pan over a low heat for 15 minutes. Add the zucchini, mixed herbs and black olives, cook for another 5 minutes, then add the basil.

Grill the sausages for about 10 minutes, or until well browned and cooked through. Warm the buns in the oven for 5 minutes.

Open the buns, add the sausages and top with the eggplant stew. Close the buns and serve immediately.

CAPRI

CHIPOLATA, CAPERBERRIES, CUCUMBER
TOMATO PESTO

makes 4 hot dogs

4 milk buns (see page 128)
4 chipolata sausages
1 cucumber
4 tablespoons caster (superfine) sugar
4 tablespoons rice vinegar
150 g (5½ oz) semi-dried (sun-blushed) tomatoes in oil
4 tablespoons olive oil
80 g (2¾ oz) grated parmesan cheese
1 teaspoon Espelette chilli powder (see **note**)
Salt and pepper
100 g (3½ oz) snow peas (mangetout)
8 caperberries with their stems, halved lengthways

Note: Espelette chilli powder is a mild and fruity chilli powder from the Basque region, available from speciality food stores. You can substitute with sweet paprika and chilli powder in a 3:1 ratio.

Preheat the oven to 160°C (315°F/Gas 2–3).

Quarter the cucumber lengthways and remove the seeds then slice thinly. Combine the slices with the sugar and rice vinegar and cover with water.

In a food processor, make a pesto with the semi-dried tomatoes, olive oil, parmesan cheese and chilli powder. Season.

Drop the snow peas into boiling salted water for 5 minutes. Rinse them immediately under cold water and slice on an angle.

Grill the sausages for about 10 minutes, or until well browned and cooked through. Warm the buns in the oven for 5 minutes.

Open the buns, add the sausages, top with the tomato pesto and poke in the pieces of cucumber, snow peas and caperberries. Close the buns and serve immediately.

CAPTAIN

CHIPOLATA, ANCHOVIES, GREEN MAYO, TARRAGON

makes 4 hot dogs

4 milk buns (see page 128)
4 chipolata sausages
100 g (3½ oz) snow peas (mangetout)
100 g (3½ oz) green beans, trimmed
1 bunch of tarragon, chopped
8 anchovies in oil, chopped
1 tablespoon mayonnaise
1 tablespoon moutarde de Meaux (wholegrain mustard)
100 g (3½ oz) semi-dried (sun-blushed) tomatoes, diced
50 g (1¾ oz) chorizo, diced

Preheat the oven to 160°C (315°F/Gas 2–3).

Drop the snow peas into boiling salted water for 5 minutes. Rinse immediately under cold water and slice on the diagonal.

Cook the green beans in the same way and finely chop them.

Combine the tarragon and anchovies with the mayonnaise and wholegrain mustard. Combine the mixture with the snow peas, beans, tomatoes and chorizo.

Grill the sausages for about 10 minutes, or until well browned and cooked through. Warm the buns in the oven for 5 minutes.

Open the buns, add the sausages and top with the chorizo mixture. Close the buns and serve immediately.

ROMA

makes 4 hot dogs

4 sweet milk buns (see page 128)
4 chipolata sausages
2 garlic cloves, sliced
2 white onions, sliced
4 tablespoons olive oil
2 tomatoes, chopped
2 thyme sprigs
Salt and pepper
4 coriander (cilantro) sprigs, leaves only
1 fennel bulb, tough outer layer discarded,
    remainder sliced
2 small purple artichokes, peeled and quartered

Preheat the oven to 160°C (315°F/Gas 2–3).

Sauté the garlic and onion in the olive oil over a medium–low heat for 5 minutes, add the tomato and thyme and let the mixture stew for about 5 minutes, or until saucy. Season and add the coriander leaves.

Grill the fennel and artichoke on a cast-iron plate or chargrill pan until soft and slightly charred.

Grill the sausages for about 10 minutes, or until well browned and cooked through. Warm the buns in the oven for 5 minutes.

Open the buns, add the sausages, top with the stewed tomato and the grilled fennel and artichoke. Close the buns and serve immediately.

The Merguez

Merguez is the exotic member of the coarse-ground group of sausages. From North Africa, it is made from beef and mutton and delights the most fastidious palates with its spicy piquant flavour. Cumin, pepper and chilli revive, surprise and shake up our taste buds. Traditionally fresh and grilled, the merguez loves hanging around stadiums on match nights, where it is often sold burnt—raw. It deserves more respect: it should be cooked gently so that it can brown at a leisurely pace and lose its excess fat, thus revealing all of its character.

If this sausage is not available from speciality butchers or good food markets, ask your butcher to suggest a suitable substitute.

ROCO

MERGUEZ, DRIED FRUIT, SPICES

makes 4 hot dogs

4 milk buns (see page 128)
4 merguez sausages
2 garlic cloves, sliced
2 white onions, sliced
2 tablespoons olive oil
1 teaspoon mustard seeds
1 teaspoon coriander seeds
1 teaspoon fennel seeds
1 teaspoon cumin seeds
2 tablespoons Savora sweet mustard sauce
  (see **note** page 8)
100 g (3½ oz) prunes, diced
100 g (3½ oz) dried apricots, diced

Preheat the oven to 160°C (315°F/Gas 2–3).

Sauté the garlic and onion in the olive oil in a frying pan over a low heat for 5 minutes. Add the spices, the mustard sauce, the dried fruit and a glass of water and cook the mixture over a low heat until the liquid has completely evaporated.

Grill the sausages for about 10 minutes, or until well browned and cooked through. Warm the buns in the oven for 5 minutes.

Open the buns, add the sausages and top with the dried fruit and spice mixture. Close the buns and serve immediately.

ROYAL
MERGUEZ, HARISSA, MIXED VEGETABLES RAS EL HANOUT

makes 4 hot dogs

4 milk buns (see page 128)
4 merguez sausages
2 white onions, chopped
2 garlic cloves, crushed
50 g (1¾ oz/¼ cup) chopped fresh ginger
2 parsnips, cut into batons
2 carrots, cut into batons
2 tomatoes, diced
60 ml (2 fl oz/¼ cup) vegetable stock
1 tablespoon ras el hanout (see **note**)
1 tablespoon harissa
6 chives, finely chopped

Note: Ras el hanout is a spice mix from North Africa, available from speciality food stores.

Preheat the oven to 160°C (315°F/Gas 2–3).
Sauté the onion, garlic and ginger in the olive oil in a saucepan over a medium–low heat for 5 minutes, or until softened. Add the parsnip, carrot, tomato, vegetable stock and the ras el hanout and let this mixture cook for a further 12 minutes until the vegetables are well cooked.
Remove the vegetables, and continue cooking the stock over a high heat for 2–3 minutes, or until the sauce is syrupy and reduced. Add the harissa. Glaze the vegetables with some of this sauce and reserve the rest.
Grill the sausages for about 10 minutes, or until well browned and cooked through. Warm the buns in the oven for 5 minutes.
Open the buns, spread with the reserved sauce, add the sausages, top with the mixed vegetables and sprinkle with chives. Close the buns and serve immediately.

PATATE

MERGUEZ, POTATO, PINE NUTS
CURRY SAUCE

makes 4 hot dogs

4 sweet milk buns (see page 128)
4 merguez sausages
4 garlic cloves, finely chopped
10 g (¼ oz) fresh ginger, finely chopped
2 white onions, finely chopped
100 g (3½ oz/⅔ cup) pine nuts
3 tablespoons sunflower oil
1 apple, peeled, cored and diced
1 potato, cooked and diced
1 little gem (sucrine) or baby cos lettuce,
 leaves separated
1 teaspoon curry powder
1 pinch cinnamon
1 teaspoon honey
1 teaspoon mild mustard
Salt and pepper

Preheat the oven to 160°C (315°F/Gas 2–3).

Sauté the garlic, ginger, onion and pine nuts in the sunflower oil over a medium heat for 2 minutes until lightly browned. Add the apple, potato, lettuce leaves, curry powder, cinnamon, honey and mustard. Season, then cook for 5 minutes until the apple and potato are cooked through.

Grill the sausages for about 10 minutes, or until well browned and cooked through. Warm the buns in the oven for 5 minutes.

Open the buns, add the sausages and top with the apple and potato mixture. Close the buns and serve immediately.

IZNOGOUD

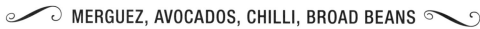

MERGUEZ, AVOCADOS, CHILLI, BROAD BEANS

makes 4 hot dogs

4 milk buns (see page 128)
4 merguez sausages
200 g (7 oz) broad beans, podded
2 avocados, peeled and stones removed
Juice of 1 lemon
4 tablespoons olive oil
2 tomatoes, diced
1 French shallot (eschalot), finely chopped
1 bird's eye chilli, finely chopped
4 chives, finely chopped
Salt and pepper

Preheat the oven to 160°C (315°F/Gas 2–3).

Drop the broad beans into boiling salted water for
30 seconds and immediately rinse under cold water.
Slip off their skins.

In a food processor, roughly process the avocados
with the lemon juice and olive oil then combine with the
tomato, broad beans, shallot, chilli and chives. Season.

Grill the sausages for about 10 minutes, or until well
browned and cooked through. Warm the buns in the oven
for 5 minutes.

Open the buns, add the sausages and top with the
avocado mixture. Close the buns and serve immediately.

The Montbéliard

This is one of the oldest known varieties, the grandmother of our sausages. Curved in shape with a lovely amber hue, it is made from coarsely ground pork seasoned with cumin, pepper and other flavourings that vary according to the butcher. With its smoky flavour, the poached sausage literally explodes when you bite into it, offering a multitude of flavours in the mouth. This sausage is only made in Franche-Comté, but it is enjoyed everywhere good things are appreciated. The Montbéliard is similar to a Morteau but slightly smaller and less smoked. It has a real personality that sets it apart from its colleagues, and is able to communicate all of its sensations, even its feelings.

If this sausage is not available from speciality butchers or good food markets, ask your butcher to suggest a well-flavoured pork sausage as a substitute.

DOUBCE

MONTBÉLIARD, AGED DRY-CURED HAM
AGED COMTÉ CHEESE, SHALLOTS

makes 4 hot dogs

4 milk buns (see page 128)

4 Montbéliard sausages

3 slices of dry-cured ham, aged 12 months,
   cut into thin matchsticks

150 g (5½ oz) Comté cheese, aged 12 months
   or gruyère cheese, cut into thin matchsticks

2 French shallots (eschalots), cut into thin matchsticks

1 tablespoon mild mustard

2 tablespoons olive oil

½ teaspoon turmeric

½ teaspoon paprika

1 tablespoon moutarde de Meaux (wholegrain mustard)

Preheat the oven to 160°C (315°F/Gas 2–3).

Combine the ham, Comté and shallot with the mild mustard, olive oil and spices.

Poach the sausages in gently simmering water for 10 minutes.

Open the buns and warm them in the oven for 5 minutes. Spread with the wholegrain mustard, add the sausages and top with the ham mixture. Close the buns and serve immediately.

GREEN

MONTBÉLIARD, BROAD BEANS, RADICCHIO
ESCARGOT SAUCE

makes 4 hot dogs

4 sweet milk buns (see page 128)
4 Montbéliard sausages
2 garlic cloves, finely chopped
1 bunch of curly-leaf parsley, finely chopped
150 g (5½ oz) broad beans, podded
3 white onions, sliced
60 g (2¼ oz) butter
1 tablespoon canola oil
2 heads of radicchio, finely shredded
Salt and pepper

80

Preheat the oven to 160°C (315°F/Gas 2–3).

Mix the garlic with the parsley.

Drop the broad beans into boiling salted water for
30 seconds and immediately rinse under cold water.
Slip off their skins.

Sauté the onion in the butter and canola oil in a frying
pan over a low heat for 5 minutes, or until well softened.
Add the garlic and parsley, and let the mixture cook gently
for 2 minutes. Add the radicchio and broad beans and
continue cooking for 5 minutes. Season.

Poach the sausages in gently simmering water for
10 minutes. Warm the buns in the oven for 5 minutes.

Open the buns, add the sausages and top with the broad
bean mixture. Close the buns and serve immediately.

BRUTUS

MONTBÉLIARD, TOMATOES, ONIONS, HERBS, LEMON

makes 4 hot dogs

4 sweet milk buns (see page 128)
4 Montbéliard sausages
2 bulb spring onions (scallions)
2 tablespoons sweet relish (see page 140)
2 tablespoons olive oil
2 coriander (cilantro) sprigs, roughly chopped
6 basil leaves, roughly chopped
2 oxheart tomatoes, diced
Zest and juice of 1 lemon
Salt and pepper

Preheat the oven to 160°C (315°F/Gas 2–3).
    Slice the bulb of the spring onions into thin rings and finely chop the green section.
    Combine the relish with the olive oil and herbs. Set aside a third of this mixture. Combine the remainder with the onion, tomato, lemon zest and juice. Season.
    Poach the sausages in gently simmering water for 10 minutes. Warm the buns in the oven for 5 minutes.
    Open the buns, spread with the reserved sauce, add the sausages and top with the tomato mixture. Close the buns and serve immediately.

BIQUET

MONTBÉLIARD, GOAT'S CHEESE, ROCKET

makes 4 hot dogs

4 milk buns (see page 128)
4 Montbéliard sausages
1 tablespoon honey
3 tablespoons moutarde de Meaux (wholegrain mustard)
1 tablespoon Melfor or cider vinegar (see **note**)
1 handful of rocket (arugula)
2 tablespoons olive oil
3 crottins de Chavignol or any soft-rind goat's cheese,
  thinly sliced

Note: Melfor vinegar is a herb and honey flavoured vinegar. If you can't find
it, use a cider vinegar sweetened with honey.

Preheat the oven to 160°C (315°F/Gas 2–3).
   Combine the honey, mustard and vinegar. Dress the
rocket with the olive oil.
   Poach the sausages in gently simmering water for
10 minutes.
   Open the buns, spread with the mustard mixture, add
the sausages on one side and top with some goat's
cheese. Place the remaining cheese on the other side of
the bun.
   Warm the filled buns in the oven for 5 minutes then top
with the rocket. Close the buns and serve immediately.

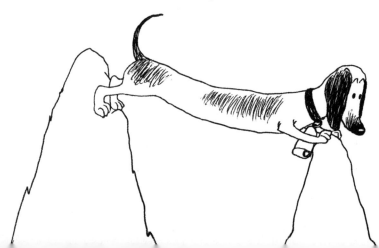

The Morteau

With the Morteau, a native of the plateaus and mountains of the Haut-Doubs and Jura, we have reached new heights. This sumo wrestler of Montbéliard sausages is made from pork and smoked over pinewoods and juniper in the Morteau region—to transform a pink and well-larded body into one that's golden and … well-larded. For once, smoking is a source of beauty and goodness! This sausage can be recognised by its fetching wooden pendant featuring the insignia of its manufacturer. It is cooked whole in a large saucepan. All that's left is to cut yourself a generous slice and indulge.

If this sausage is not available from speciality butchers or good food markets, ask your butcher to suggest a well-spiced and strong flavoured pork sausage as a substitute.

ROOTS
MORTEAU, CHESTNUTS, CHORIZO
BRUSSELS SPROUTS

makes 4 hot dogs

4 milk buns (see page 128)
2 small Morteau sausages
1 tablespoon mild mustard
1 teaspoon worcestershire sauce
1 teaspoon soy sauce
1 tablespoon canola oil
100 g (3½ oz) spicy chorizo, cut into thin matchsticks
1 tablespoon olive oil
½ a bunch of flat-leaf (Italian) parsley, roughly chopped
100 g (3½ oz) cooked chestnuts (see **note**)
100 g (3½ oz) brussels sprouts, leaves separated
1 mild red chilli, sliced

Note: Cooked and peeled chestnuts are available in vacuum packets from speciality food stores.

Preheat the oven to 160°C (315°F/Gas 2–3).

Combine the mustard, worcestershire sauce, soy sauce and canola oil.

Pan-fry the chorizo in the olive oil with the parsley, chestnuts, brussels sprouts and chilli for 3–4 minutes over a low heat.

Poach the sausages in gently simmering water for 10 minutes and slice into rounds. Warm the buns in the oven for 5 minutes.

Open the buns, spread with the sauce, add the sausage rounds and top with the chorizo mixture. Close the buns and serve immediately.

BLUEBERRY

MORTEAU, COMTÉ, BLUEBERRY SAUCE, TARRAGON

makes 4 hot dogs

4 sweet milk buns (see page 128)
2 small Morteau sausages
150 g (5½ oz) frozen blueberries
2 tablespoons balsamic vinegar
2 tablespoons light brown sugar
1 garlic clove, finely chopped
3 tablespoons olive oil
150 g (5½ oz) mature Comté or gruyère cheese,
　thinly sliced
2 tarragon sprigs, leaves only

Preheat the oven to 160°C (315°F/Gas 2–3).

Cook the blueberries in a saucepan with the balsamic vinegar and brown sugar over a low heat for 15 minutes.

Gently sauté the garlic in the olive oil over a low heat for 1 minute.

Poach the sausages in gently simmering water for 10 minutes and slice into rounds.

Open the buns, brush them with the garlic olive oil and add the sausage slices, tucking slices of Comté in between them.

Warm the filled buns in the oven for 5 minutes, then top with the blueberry sauce and tarragon leaves. Close the buns and serve immediately.

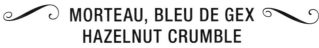

CHEEEESE

MORTEAU, BLEU DE GEX
HAZELNUT CRUMBLE

makes 4 hot dogs

4 sweet milk buns (see page 128)
2 small Morteau sausages
50 g (1¾ oz) hazelnuts, roughly chopped
50 g (1¾ oz/⅓ cup) plain (all-purpose) flour
50 g (1¾ oz) butter
30 g (1 oz) light brown sugar
2 tablespoons quince jelly
150 g (5½ oz) bleu de Gex or other creamy blue cheese,
    thinly sliced

Preheat the oven to 180°C (350°F/Gas 4).
    Combine the hazelnuts, flour, butter and sugar in an
ovenproof dish and bake in the oven for 15 minutes, or
until the crumble is golden brown. Remove from the oven
and reduce the temperature to 160°C (315°F/Gas 2–3).
    Poach the sausages in gently simmering water for
10 minutes then slice into rounds.
    Open the buns, spread with the quince jelly, add the
sausage slices and top with the blue cheese.
    Warm the filled buns in the oven for 5 minutes then
sprinkle with the crumble. Close the buns and serve
immediately.

MOMO

MORTEAU, SCRAMBLED EGGS WITH MORELS

makes 4 hot dogs

4 milk buns (see page 128)
2 small Morteau sausages
30 g (1 oz) dried morel mushroom pieces (see **note**)
4 eggs
1 tablespoon crème fraîche
1 bunch of chives, finely chopped
Salt and pepper
50 g (1¾ oz) butter
1 garlic clove, halved
1 tomato, halved

Note: Dried morel mushrooms are available from speciality food stores.

Preheat the oven to 160°C (315°F/Gas 2–3).

Simmer the morel pieces in water for 10 minutes then drain.

Whisk the eggs, then add the crème fraîche and chives and season.

Poach the sausages in gently simmering water for 10 minutes then slice into rounds.

In a non-stick frying pan, sauté the sausage pieces in the butter over a medium heat until lightly browned, then add the morel and egg mixture. Cook until the mixture looks somewhere between scrambled eggs and an omelette.

Open the buns, rub them with the garlic and the tomato halves and warm them in the oven for 5 minutes. Fill the buns with the sausage mix. Close the buns and serve immediately.

The Toulouse Sausage

As its name suggests, this sausage sings the songs of Claude Nougaro, regularly raises the Brennus Shield, melts under the red brick of the Minimes stadium, has a seductive accent and can take an assault of Tarbais beans without complaint. Traditionally pork, fresh and uncooked, it is called a 'Banger' or a 'Snag' in the UK. It is the sexiest of sausages and enjoys a wealth of affection on a national level. The Toulouse is a robust customer with broad shoulders, variable size and a thick skin that can survive simmering water for 10 minutes, accept hot embers without flinching and take a good branding. The Toulouse sausage is as manly as a Dieux du Stade calendar, but much more palatable.

If this sausage is not available from speciality butchers or good food markets, ask your butcher for advice or substitute with an Italian pork sausage.

MATCH

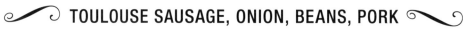 **TOULOUSE SAUSAGE, ONION, BEANS, PORK**

makes 4 hot dogs

1 baguette, cut into 4
4 Toulouse sausages
3 white onions, sliced
3 slices of pork belly, cut into small chunks
1 tablespoon duck fat
1 tomato, diced
1 teaspoon tomato paste (concentrated purée)
200 g (7 oz) cooked white beans (leftover cassoulet), or tinned white beans, drained and rinsed
1 tablespoon strong mustard

Preheat the oven to 160°C (315°F/Gas 2–3).

Sauté the onion and pork belly in the duck fat over a medium heat for 5 minutes. Add the tomato and tomato paste and cook for about 10 minutes, or until well cooked. Add the beans and warm through.

Grill the sausages for about 10 minutes, or until well browned and cooked through. Warm the baguette pieces in the oven for 5 minutes.

Open up the pieces of baguette, spread with the mustard, then add the sausages and top with the beans and pork. Close the buns and serve immediately.

PISTACHIO

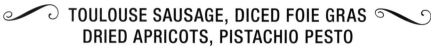

TOULOUSE SAUSAGE, DICED FOIE GRAS
DRIED APRICOTS, PISTACHIO PESTO

makes 4 hot dogs

4 traditional hot dog buns (see page 128)
4 Toulouse sausages
10 dried apricots, diced
2 tablespoons Armagnac
100 g (3½ oz/¾ cup) pistachios
4 tablespoons olive oil
1 handful of rocket (arugula)
Salt and pepper
2 slices of fresh foie gras, diced

Preheat the oven to 160°C (315°F/Gas 2–3).

Place the apricot and Armagnac in a saucepan, cover with water and bring to the boil. Remove from the heat and set aside for 15 minutes.

In a food processor, make a pesto with three-quarters of the pistachios, the olive oil and the rocket. Season.

Brown the foie gras in a very hot frying pan with no added fat. Drain on paper towel. Season.

Sauté the apricot in the same pan using the fat from the foie gras. Cook over a low heat for 2–3 minutes.

Grill the sausages for about 10 minutes, or until well browned and cooked through. Warm the buns in the oven for 5 minutes.

Open the buns, spread with the pistachio pesto, add the sausages, and top with the foie gras, apricot and the remaining pistachios. Close the buns and serve immediately.

BOGA

TOULOUSE SAUSAGE, FRESH HERBS, BACON BARBECUE SAUCE

makes 4 hot dogs

4 sweet milk buns (see page 128)
4 Toulouse sausages
4 thin slices of smoked bacon
1 bunch of flat-leaf (Italian) parsley, leaves only
1 bunch of basil, leaves only
1 bunch of coriander (cilantro), leaves only
1 bulb spring onion (scallion), sliced
2 tablespoons olive oil
4 tablespoons barbecue sauce (see page 138)
1 handful of young mustard greens

Preheat the oven to 160°C (315°F/Gas 2–3).

Wrap the sausages in the bacon.

Combine the herbs with the onion and dress with the olive oil.

Grill the sausages for about 10 minutes, or until well browned and cooked through. Warm the buns in the oven for 5 minutes.

Open the buns, spread with the barbecue sauce, add the sausages and top with the herb mixture and mustard greens. Close the buns and serve immediately.

JACKY

TOULOUSE SAUSAGE, PIPERADE, HAZELNUTS

makes 4 hot dogs

1 baguette, cut into 4
4 Toulouse sausages
3 red capsicums (peppers), sliced into thin strips
3 white onions, sliced
3 tomatoes, diced
4 garlic cloves, sliced
1 teaspoon Espelette chilli powder (see **note** page 60)
4 tablespoons olive oil
Salt and pepper
50 g (1¾ oz) hazelnuts

Preheat the oven to 160°C (315°F/Gas 2–3).

To make the piperade, sauté the capsicum, onion, tomato, garlic and chilli powder in the olive oil in a frying pan over a low heat for 20 minutes. Season.

Grill the sausages for about 10 minutes, or until well browned and cooked through. Warm the baguette pieces in the oven for 5 minutes.

Open up the baguette pieces, add the sausages, top with the piperade and the hazelnuts. Close the buns and serve immediately.

The Diot

'Star of the snows, my amorous heart is caught in the trap of your beautiful … diots', the song could go. The Savoie gave birth to these small, smoked nutmeg-scented pork sausages. Also known as the Savoy, the diot takes on different looks and flavours according to its variety: plain, with cabbage or smoked, with herbs—there are as many diots as butchers. The diot can cook on the grill, bubble in a broth or get drunk on white wine. For a pleasure that really hits the spot, enjoy them rough and ready, schuss-style.

If this sausage is not available from speciality butchers or good food markets, ask your butcher for advice or substitute with an Italian pork sausage.

SCHUSS

DIOT, REBLOCHON CHEESE, PORK BELLY, SORREL

makes 4 hotdogs

4 sweet milk buns (see page 128)
4 diot sausages
2 slices of pork belly, cut into small chunks or lardons
1 garlic clove, halved
a little olive oil
150 g (5½ oz) farmstead (fermier) reblochon or
    raclette cheese, diced
2 tomatoes, diced
3 sorrel leaves, shredded

Preheat the oven to 160°C (315°F/Gas 2–3).
    Brown the pork belly for 2–3 minutes in a frying pan over a medium–high heat.
    Grill the sausages for about 10 minutes, or until well browned and cooked through.
    Open the buns, rub them with the garlic halves and drizzle with a little olive oil. Add the sausages and top with the cheese, pork belly and tomato.
    Warm the filled buns in the oven for 5 minutes, then scatter over the sorrel. Close the buns and serve immediately.

BRI

DIOT, BRIE, WITLOF

makes 4 hot dogs

4 traditional hot dog buns (see page 128)
4 diot sausages
1 witlof (chicory), sliced
2 tablespoons olive oil
5 chives, finely chopped
1 tablespoon fromage blanc or quark
Salt and pepper
200 g (7 oz) brie, thinly sliced
50 g (1¾ oz) black dry-salted olives, pitted

Preheat the oven to 160°C (315°F/Gas 2–3).
    Dress the sliced witlof with 1 tablespoon of the olive oil.
    Combine the chives with the fromage blanc and the remaining tablespoon of olive oil. Season.
    Grill the sausages for about 10 minutes, or until well browned and cooked through.
    Open the buns, spread with the fromage blanc, add the sausages then top with the brie and black olives.
    Warm the filled buns in the oven for 5 minutes, then top with the witlof. Close the buns and serve immediately.

VULCANE

DIOT, LEEKS, GINGER, SWEET RELISH

makes 4 hot dogs

4 milk buns (see page 128)
4 diot sausages
3 baby (or thin) leeks, pale parts only
2 tablespoons olive oil
10 g (¼ oz) fresh ginger, chopped
3 slices of Spanish jamon (dry-cured ham) with
   a good amount of fat, chopped
2 tablespoons sweet relish (see page 140)
Sunflower oil, for deep-frying

Preheat the oven to 160°C (315°F/Gas 2–3).

Finely chop two of the leeks and sauté in a frying pan in the olive oil with the ginger and ham. Leave to cook over a low heat for 10 minutes, then add the relish.

Heat the sunflower oil for deep-frying in a small heavy-based saucepan over a medium heat. Slice the third leek lengthways and, once the oil is hot enough, deep-fry the sliced leek for 1 minute, or until lightly golden. Carefully transfer to paper towel to drain.

Grill the sausages for about 10 minutes, or until well browned and cooked through.

Open the buns, add the sautéed leeks and the sausages. Warm the filled buns in the oven for 5 minutes, then top with the deep-fried leek. Close the buns and serve immediately.

LEMON

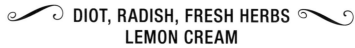

DIOT, RADISH, FRESH HERBS
LEMON CREAM

makes 4 hot dogs

4 milk buns (see page 128)
4 diot sausages
1 tablespoon crème fraîche
1 tablespoon mayonnaise
Zest and juice of 1 lemon
Fleur de sel (fine sea salt) and pepper
6 coriander (cilantro) sprigs, leaves only
2 bulb spring onions (scallions), sliced
1 bunch of radishes, thinly sliced
½ a handful of rocket (arugula) leaves
½ a handful of baby spinach leaves

Preheat the oven to 160°C (315°F/Gas 2–3).

To make the dressing, combine the crème fraîche, mayonnaise, lemon zest and juice. Season. Combine the coriander, spring onion and radish with the dressing.

Grill the sausages for about 10 minutes, or until well browned and cooked through. Warm the buns in the oven for 5 minutes.

Open the buns, add the sausages and top with the rocket and spinach leaves and the dressed radishes. Close the buns and serve immediately.

The Chicken Sausage

This sausage is a good alternative for those who prefer not to indulge in porkies but who secretly dream of the instant gratification and deep nostalgia of a hot dog. Chicken takes the place of the pork, making this lower in fat so you can put more sauce on your hot dog with a clear conscience! As the Greek philosopher Dunkhan said: 'Chicken sausage means waist control; pork sausage means belly roll!'

Cooking note: These chicken sausages are cured and ready to eat, so they only take a few minutes to reheat in simmering water. If your chicken sausages are raw, they must be cooked for longer until thoroughly cooked, and you may prefer an alternative cooking method to poaching.

FRESH

CHICKEN SAUSAGE, TOMATO TARTARE, PESTO PARMESAN, ROCKET

makes 4 hot dogs

4 milk buns (see page 128)
4 chicken sausages
120 g (4¼ oz) parmesan cheese
2 tablespoons pine nuts
1 bunch of basil
5 tablespoons olive oil
1 garlic clove
Salt and pepper
1 handful of rocket (arugula)
3 oxheart tomatoes, diced

Preheat the oven to 180°C (350°F/Gas 4).

Shave a third of the parmesan cheese using a vegetable peeler. Grate the remainder.

Toast the pine nuts in the oven for about 5 minutes. Reduce the oven temperature to 160°C (315°F/Gas 2–3).

In a food processor, make a pesto with the basil, 4 tablespoons of the olive oil, the grated parmesan and the garlic. Season.

Dress the rocket with the remaining tablespoon of olive oil.

Combine the tomato with the pesto. Add the pine nuts and shaved parmesan.

Poach the sausages in gently simmering water for 3 minutes until hot and cooked through (see note about cooking on page 116).

Warm the buns in the oven for 5 minutes.

Open the buns, spread with the pesto mixture, add the rocket and the sausages. Close the buns and serve immediately.

CÆSAR

CHICKEN SAUSAGE, COS, ANCHOVIES, PARMESAN

makes 4 hot dogs

4 traditional hot dog buns (see page 128)
4 chicken sausages
100 g (3½ oz) anchovies in oil
1 garlic clove
1 tablespoon mild mustard
4 tablespoons olive oil
2 little gem (sucrine) or baby cos lettuces,
   leaves separated
100 g (3½ oz) parmesan cheese, shaved
   with a vegetable peeler
1 red onion, thinly sliced

Preheat the oven to 160°C (315°F/Gas 2–3).

Set aside 8 whole anchovies. In a food processor, make a dressing by processing the remaining anchovies with the garlic, mustard and olive oil until smooth. Reserve half the dressing and use the remainder to dress the lettuce.

Poach the sausages in gently simmering water for 3 minutes until hot and cooked through (see note about cooking on page 116). Warm the buns in the oven for 5 minutes.

Open the buns, spread with the reserved dressing then fill with the lettuce, sausages, whole anchovies, parmesan and onion. Close the buns and serve immediately.

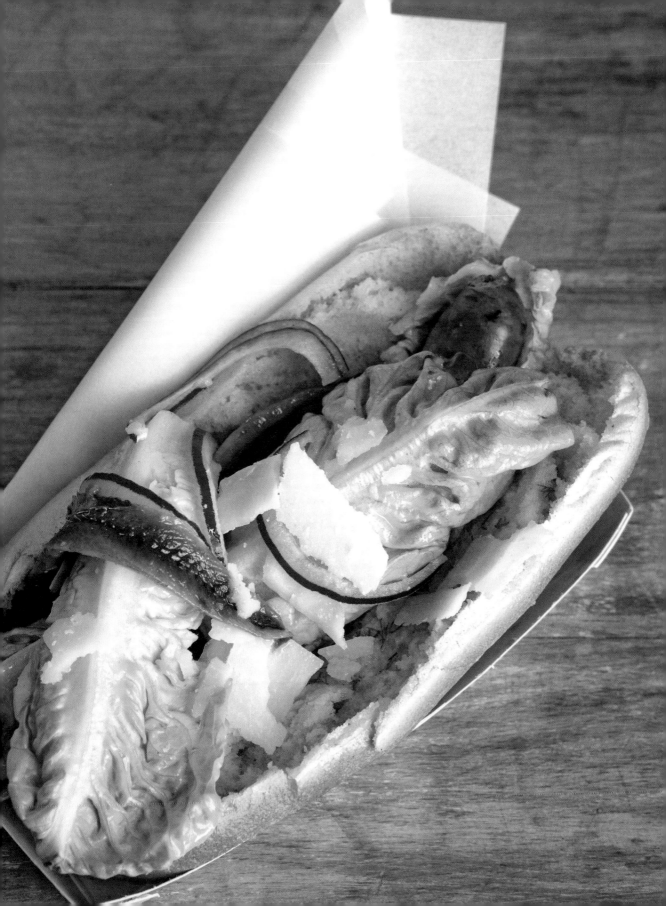

BOLLY

CHICKEN SAUSAGE, CURRY SAUCE, GRUYÈRE CREAM
DRIED FRUITS

makes 4 hot dogs

4 milk buns (see page 128)
4 chicken sausages
150 g (5½ oz/1½ cups) grated gruyère cheese
1 tablespoon crème fraîche
1 tablespoon Savora sweet mustard sauce (see **note** page 8)
8 chives, finely chopped
1 teaspoon curry powder
6 pitted prunes, diced
6 dried apricots, diced

Preheat the oven to 160°C (315°F/Gas 2–3).

Combine the cheese, crème fraîche, mustard sauce, chives, curry powder and dried fruit.

Poach the sausages in gently simmering water for 3 minutes until hot and cooked through (see note about cooking on page 116). or until piping hot and cooked through.

Open the buns, spread with the cheese mixture, add the sausages and close the bun.

Warm the filled buns in the oven for 5 minutes then serve immediately.

NENETH

CHICKEN SAUSAGE, SMOKED SALMON, DILL SPRING ONION

makes 4 hot dogs

4 milk buns (see page 128)
4 chicken sausages
1 bunch of dill, leaves only
3 tablespoons olive oil
2 tablespoons mayonnaise
1 teaspoon Savora sweet mustard sauce (see **note** page 8)
Juice of 1 lemon
1 granny smith apple, cored and thinly sliced
1 bulb spring onion (scallion), thinly sliced
150 g (5½ oz) smoked salmon, thinly sliced

Preheat the oven to 160°C (315°F/Gas 2–3).

In a food processor, finely purée half the dill leaves with the olive oil. Combine the remaining dill with the mayonnaise, mustard sauce, lemon juice, apple, spring onion and the smoked salmon.

Poach the sausages in gently simmering water for 3 minutes until hot and cooked through (see note about cooking on page 116). Warm the buns in the oven for 5 minutes.

Open the buns, brush with the dill olive oil, add the sausages and top with the smoked salmon mixture. Close the buns and serve immediately.

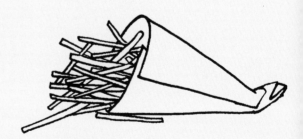

Good company for your
HOT DOGS

HOT DOG BUNS

MILK BUNS

Preparation time 20 minutes + 2 hours rising time
Cooking time 15 minutes

makes 6 buns

1 sachet (7 g/¼ oz) yeast
200 ml (7 fl oz) lukewarm milk
400 g (14 oz/2⅔ cups) T55 flour (see **note** below right)
1 teaspoon salt
1 tablespoon caster (superfine) sugar
1 egg yolk, lightly beaten

Add the yeast to the lukewarm milk.

Combine the flour, salt, sugar and the yeasty milk and knead until smooth and elastic to form a compact ball. Cover with a warm damp cloth and let the dough rise for 1 hour at room temperature.

Punch the air out of the dough, divide into 6 rolls of equal size and place these on a baking tray lined with baking paper. Cover with a warm damp cloth and let them rise again at room temperature for 1 hour.

Preheat the oven to 180°C (350°F/Gas 4).

Glaze with egg yolk and bake for 15 minutes.

Gourmet options

Before baking, sprinkle the buns with poppy seeds, sesame seeds, grated cheese ...

When kneading the dough, add small pieces of bacon, diced chorizo sausage, dried tomatoes, caramelised onions ...

SWEET MILK BUNS

1 sachet (7 g/¼ oz) yeast
150 ml (5 fl oz) lukewarm milk
350 g (12 oz/2⅓ cups) T55 flour (see **note** below)
50 g (1¾ oz) caster (superfine) sugar
75 g (2½ oz) softened butter

Proceed as for the milk bun recipe, adding the butter to the flour mixture before kneading.

TRADITIONAL (AMERICAN-STYLE) HOT DOG BUNS

1½ sachets (10 g/⅓ oz) yeast
150 ml (5 fl oz) lukewarm milk
500 g (1 lb 2 oz/3⅓ cups) T65 flour (see **note** below)
1 teaspoon salt
60 g (2¼ oz) softened butter
120 ml (4 fl oz) water

Proceed as for the milk bun recipe, adding the butter and water to the flour mixture before kneading.

Note: T55 and T65 are French flours used in making breads and baguettes. They are available from speciality stores. You can use strong flour as an alternative.

SUPER FRIES

makes 1 serve

300 g (10½ oz) bintje (yellow finn) potatoes per person
   (see **note**)
Sunflower oil, for deep-frying
Salt

Note: Bintje is a waxy potato ideal for making fries and is widely available.

Peel the potatoes (or leave them unpeeled). Cut them into
1 cm (½ inch) chips. Rinse the chips and dry them (this is
an important step for crispness).
   Heat the sunflower oil in a deep-fryer or large heavy-
based saucepan to 170°C (325°F), or until a cube
of bread dropped into the oil turns golden brown in
20 seconds.
   Deep-fry the chips for 5 minutes. Remove from the oil
for 10 minutes and set the oil to one side during that time.
   Reheat the oil and return the chips to the oil. Cook until
golden brown. Drain on paper towel. Season (use paprika
or curry powder ... for something different) and serve
immediately.

STRAW POTATOES

makes 1 serve

300 g (10½ oz) bintje (yellow finn) potatoes per person
  (see **note** on page 130)
Sunflower oil, for deep-frying
Salt

Peel the potatoes and slice them thinly with a mandoline.
Cut the slices into thin matchsticks. Rinse the slices and dry
them (an important step for crispness).

Heat the sunflower oil in a deep-fryer or large heavy-
based saucepan to 170°C (325°F), or until a cube
of bread dropped into the oil turns golden brown in
20 seconds.

Deep-fry the straws, stirring them with a slotted spoon,
for 3–4 minutes, or until they are golden brown.

Remove the straws from the oil and drain on paper
towel. Season and serve immediately.

HOUSE POTATO CRISPS

makes 1 serve

300 g (10½ oz) bintje (yellow finn, or vitelotte or
    purple congo for the colour) potatoes per person
    (see **note** on page 130)
Sunflower oil, for deep-frying
Salt

Peel the potatoes and slice them thinly with
a mandoline. Rinse the slices and dry them
(an important step for crispness).

Heat the sunflower oil in a deep-fryer or large
heavy-based saucepan to 170°C (325°F),
or until a cube of bread dropped into the oil
turns golden brown in 20 seconds.

Deep-fry the potatoes for 5 minutes. Remove
from the oil and drain on paper towel. Season.
Store the crisps in an airtight container.

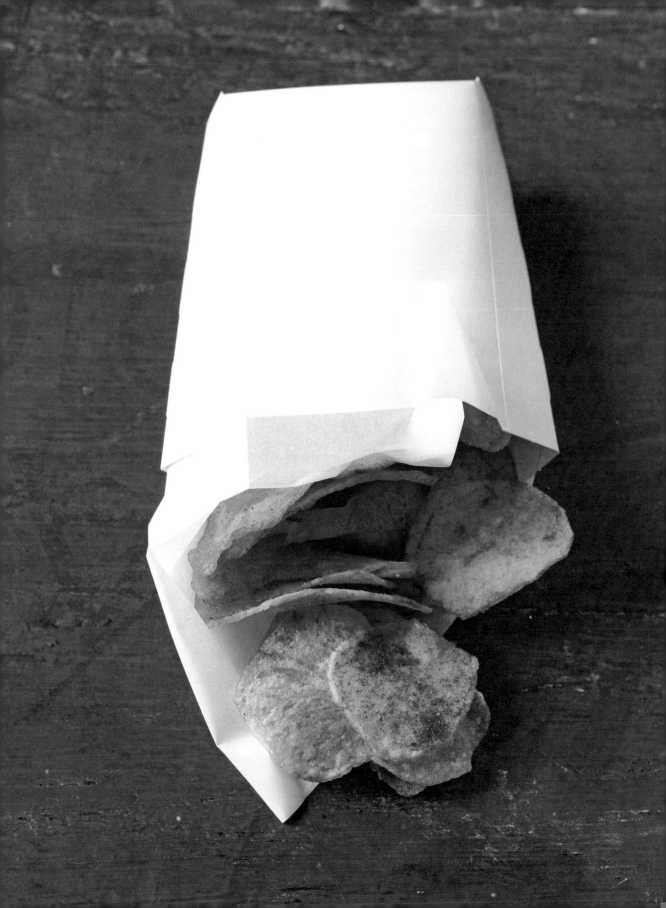

ONION RINGS

makes 4 serves

150 g (5½ oz/1 cup) plain (all-purpose) flour
1 tablespoon Espelette chilli powder (see **note** page 60)
1 teaspoon salt
Sunflower oil, for deep-frying
4 large white onions, cut into 5 mm (¼ inch) rings
2 eggs, lightly beaten

Combine the flour, chilli powder and salt.

Heat the sunflower oil in a deep-fryer or large heavy-based saucepan to 170°C (325°F), or until a cube of bread dropped into the oil turns golden brown in 20 seconds.

Dip the onion rings in the egg, let any excess drip off and then toss in the flour mixture until completely coated.

Deep-fry the onion for 3–5 minutes, or until they are golden brown. Drain on paper towel then serve immediately while they are crispy.

KETCHUP & CO
HOME-MADE

A good sauce made with choice ingredients is enough to make a bit of bread with a sausage on it unique. We leave behind the supermarket shelves and their mass-produced wares, take out our knives, put on an apron and launch into the kitchen ... We dress our hot dogs and watch for the reactions of our guests, in case we're in for a dressing down!

KETCHUP

800 g (1 lb 12 oz) well-ripened tomatoes
5 g (⅛ oz) fresh ginger, chopped
2 garlic cloves, chopped
2 tablespoons honey
80 g (2¾ oz) light brown sugar
½ teaspoon ground cumin
½ teaspoon ground cinnamon
1 tablespoon white wine vinegar

Drop the tomatoes into boiling water for 10 seconds, then drain, allow to cool and remove their skins. Seed the tomatoes and dice the flesh.

Combine all the ingredients in a saucepan and cook over a low heat for 45 minutes, stirring regularly. Purée the mixture and store in the refrigerator.

PESTO CLASSICO

100 g (3½ oz/⅔ cup) pine nuts
2 bunches of basil, leaves only
2 garlic cloves, crushed
100 g (3½ oz) parmesan cheese, diced
Juice of 1 lemon
200 ml (7 fl oz) olive oil (or more, depending on the consistency you want)
Salt and pepper

Preheat the oven to 180°C (350°F/Gas 4). Toast the pine nuts in the oven for 5 minutes, or until golden brown. In a food processor, make a pesto with the pine nuts, basil, garlic, parmesan and lemon juice, slowly adding the olive oil until it has the desired consistency. Season.

BARBECUE SAUCE

2 sweet onions, finely chopped
4 garlic cloves, finely chopped
2 tablespoons olive oil
3 tablespoons tomato paste (concentrated purée)
3 tablespoons ketchup (the one above of course)
1 tablespoon mild mustard
2 tablespoons worcestershire sauce
2 tablespoons wine vinegar
100 ml (3½ fl oz) white wine
100 ml (3½ fl oz) vegetable stock
1 tablespoon molasses

Sauté the onion and garlic in the olive oil over a low heat until softened. Add the remaining ingredients and cook for 45 minutes. Purée the mixture and store in the refrigerator.

KETCHUP & CO
HOME-MADE

SWEET RELISH

2 cucumbers, peeled and diced
3 white onions, diced
3 yellow capsicums (peppers), diced
1 mild green chilli, diced
2 celery stalks, diced
Coarse salt
200 g (7 oz) pearl sugar (see **note**)
200 ml (7 fl oz) white vinegar
1 teaspoon mustard seeds
1 teaspoon celery seeds

Note: Pearl sugar is available from speciality food stores.

Sprinkle the cucumber, onion, capsicum, chilli and celery generously with salt. Leave in a strainer for 1 hour. Rinse thoroughly, and put into a saucepan with the remaining ingredients. Cook over a low heat for 1 hour, or until the mixture has a jam-like consistency. Allow to cool then store in the refrigerator.

LIKE A VIRGIN (SAUCE VIERGE)

3 tomatoes
3 bulb spring onions (scallions), thinly sliced
1 lemongrass stem, pale part only, chopped
20 g (¾ oz) fresh ginger, chopped
1 mild red chilli, thinly sliced
150 ml (5 fl oz) olive oil
Shiso sprouts
Salt and pepper

Drop the tomatoes into boiling water for 10 seconds then drain, allow to cool and remove their skins. Dice the flesh.
    Combine everything with the olive oil, add some shiso sprouts and season. Serve immediately.

TOMATO PESTO

200 g (7 oz) semi-dried (sun-blushed) tomatoes in oil
1 teaspoon ground cumin
100 g (3½ oz) parmesan cheese, diced
1 teaspoon Espelette chilli powder (see **note** page 60)
150 ml (5 fl oz) olive oil
Salt and pepper
1 French shallot (eschalot), finely chopped

In a food processor, make a pesto with the tomato, cumin, parmesan and chilli powder, slowly adding the olive oil until it has the desired consistency. Season and add the chopped shallot.

SALADS

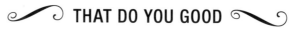

THAT DO YOU GOOD

COLESLAW WITH A DIFFERENCE

50 g (1¾ oz) raisins
125 g (4½ oz) Greek-style yoghurt
1 teaspoon dijon mustard
2 tablespoons olive oil
1 tablespoon rice vinegar
1 dill sprig, chopped
400 g (14 oz) bok choy, finely shredded
Salt and pepper

Scald the raisins to plump them up.
   Combine the yoghurt and mustard, then mix in the olive oil and vinegar. Add the raisins and dill. Season the bok choy with this dressing and serve immediately.

VEGETABLE SALAD

100 g (3½ oz/⅔ cup) shelled peas
4 tablespoons olive oil
Juice of 1 lemon
1 tablespoon maple syrup
8 mint leaves, chopped
Salt and pepper
1 fennel bulb, tough outer layer discarded, remainder
   thinly sliced
½ a bunch of radishes, thinly sliced
½ a cucumber, cut lengthways, seeds removed, then
   thinly sliced
1 small zucchini (courgette), cut lengthways, seeds
   removed, then thinly sliced
1 bulb spring onion (scallion), thinly sliced
1 mild chilli, thinly sliced
½ a bunch of chives, chopped

Drop the peas into boiling salted water for 15 seconds and rinse them immediately under cold water.
   Combine the olive oil and lemon juice, then mix in the maple syrup. Add the mint and season. Combine everything together and serve immediately.

CLASSIC SALAD

Use a mix of seasonal salad leaves, seeking out new flavours (mustard greens, mizuna, ice plant ...) and add baby spinach, diced beetroot (beet).

HERB SALAD

A bouquet of taste sensations that should explode in the mouth with well-defined flavours. It is essential for the herbs you use to be extremely fresh. All herbs are welcome (basil, tarragon, dill, sorrel, mint ...). Don't hesitate to add some baby shiso, which gives little bursts of unusual flavour.

TOP FOUR VINAIGRETTES

Simply whisk together and serve.

4 tablespoons sunflower oil
1 tablespoon sherry vinegar
1 teaspoon honey
1 teaspoon chopped French
   shallot (eschalot)
1 teaspoon dijon mustard

4 tablespoons olive oil
1 tablespoon chopped walnuts
1 teaspoon tomato sauce
   (ketchup) (see page 138)
1 teaspoon balsamic glaze
1 teaspoon Maggi seasoning
   sauce

2 tablespoons walnut oil
2 tablespoons sunflower oil
1 tablespoon balsamic vinegar
1 tablespoon moutarde
   de Meaux (wholegrain
   mustard)

4 tablespoons olive oil
½ teaspoon ground cumin
1 teaspoon lemon juice
1 teaspoon caster (superfine)
   sugar
½ teaspoon chopped garlic

Published in 2014 by Murdoch Books, an imprint of Allen & Unwin.
First published by Marabout in 2013.

Murdoch Books Australia
83 Alexander Street
Crows Nest NSW 2065
Phone: +61 (0) 2 8425 0100
Fax: +61 (0) 2 9906 2218
www.murdochbooks.com.au
info@murdochbooks.com.au

Murdoch Books UK
Erico House, 6th Floor
93–99 Upper Richmond Road
Putney, London SW15 2TG
Phone: +44 (0) 20 8785 5995
Fax: +44 (0) 20 8785 5985
www.murdochbooks.co.uk
info@murdochbooks.co.uk

For Corporate Orders & Custom Publishing contact
Noel Hammond, National Business Development Manager, Murdoch Books Australia

Publisher: Corinne Roberts
Photographer: Marie-Pierre Morel
Illustrations: José Reis De Matos
Translator: Melissa McMahon
Food editor: Michelle Earl
Editor: Victoria Chance
Editorial manager: Katie Bosher
Production: Mary Bjelobrk

A cataloguing-in-publication entry is available from the catalogue of the National Library of Australia at www.nla.gov.au.

A catalogue record for this book is available from the British Library.

Colour reproduction by Splitting Image, Clayton, Victoria.

Printed by 1010 Printing

IMPORTANT: Those who might be at risk from the effects of salmonella poisoning (the elderly, pregnant women, young children and those suffering from immune deficiency diseases) should consult their doctor with any concerns about eating raw eggs.

OVEN GUIDE: You may find cooking times vary depending on the oven you are using. For fan-forced ovens, as a general rule, set the oven temperature to 20°C (35°F) lower than indicated in the recipe.

MEASURES GUIDE: We have used 20 ml (4 teaspoon) tablespoon measures. If you are using a 15 ml (3 teaspoon) tablespoon add an extra teaspoon of the ingredient for each tablespoon specified.